How to Make $3,300 Per Month Writing E-books

T.B. McHatchins

Copyright © 2016 T.B. McHatchins

All rights reserved.

ISBN: **1540835626**
ISBN-13: **978-1540835628**

DEDICATION

To all affected by autism and mental illness.

CONTENTS

	Acknowledgments	1
1	Choosing a Niche Subject	3
2	Choosing the Perfect Title	12
3	Layout of Book	26
4	The Perfect Cover	39
5	Back Matter Description	50
6	How to Sell Your E-book	59
7	Kindle Select	69
	About the Author	74
	Bibliography	77

ACKNOWLEDGMENTS

I would like to thank my friends and family for making this a possibility for me.

1 CHOOSING A NICHE SUBJECT

When you first begin your career as an author writing E-books it is extremely important that you choose a niche subject that is popular to write about. It is just as important that you as the author are interested in the subject that you are writing about and have a passion for writing about your topic. If you do not have a passion for writing about the topic you choose the chances are going to be greater that your story will be boring and the reader will be able to tell that you were not passionate about your story.

Whether you like sports or animals it does not matter if it is a niche subject and you are totally into it and very passionate about it. It helps you to come up with more to write about if you have a passion for it. You can provide a lot more in depth details and you will have enough research to be able to get out there and really put together a good length book between 5,000 and 10,000 words.

If you are just now writing your first book, please keep in mind that it takes time to make money. The key is quality of book plus quantity of books that you have out on the market. Common sense tells us the more books that we have on the market the greater our chance of profiting and making money from the books is, however, this is only accurate if all the books are well written and of good quality for the reader to read.

When I choose a subject to write about like autism or making money online writing E-books it is a subject that I am very passionate about. I know that if I am passionate about it that I am going to make an amazing amount of money and if I do not make as much money as I had hoped I will still be okay with that because I could have funning writing my book.

I highly recommend doing some google searches over topics that you might want to write about and see how popular the topics are that you are choosing to write about. It may also be a good idea to get onto Amazon and do some searching on there to see how many books have been written on the topic and maybe purchase one so you can see what the quality of the book is. You really do want to be a fluent writer and have an awesome quality book. Some people will buy your book if it is not a good quality book but they may not recommend your book to others or post a positive review to Amazon for you. I feel it is very crucial that you put a lot of time and effort into checking your book for errors. It is simple to run a simple spelling and grammar check with Microsoft word.

There are so many good books out there about autism it could be a tough subject to compete in but because I have autism I can write very informative books that people like to read. I love to help educate others about autism so I am extremely passionate about my subject and I have built up a solid fan base off social networking sites like Facebook and Twitter. A lot of my books sell well on Amazon and I am proud of my work.

Now I am hoping to help you get started on your E-book journey as well to help you make a lot of money through passive income by only writing a story once and then watching the income come in from your excellent story.

Your passion will show in your writing. You can tell a person's passion just like you can read it in a person's voice when they are singing. Song writers write songs that they are passionate about and work hard to perfect them. It works the same when writing books. You should always keep writing about things you are passionate about. If you are not passionate about a subject, then it becomes too much like you are doing homework and you will not be successful at writing E-books because people will pick up on the fact that you are not really interested in what you are writing about.

So, to wrap up this chapter remember to always pick something that is popular or a niche subject and be sure to pick a topic to write about that you are passionate about and know something about. Your passion needs to shine through in your writing. The passion is what will sell the book.

2 CHOOSING THE PERFECT TITLE

The next step in preparing your E-book for publication is to pick a catchy title. There are several things that go into picking a title. Obviously, the title will need to have words in it that are related to the topic that you are talking about. If you are writing a book on autism spectrum disorder it makes good sense that the word autism needs to be somewhere in the title so that people know that your book is talking about autism.

If you are writing a book about making money, then you would need to make sure that you have something about the word money in the title so that the readers and customers know that your book is about making money.

A nice trick to use when titling your book is to pick a short title. Short titles are more catchy and easier for people to type in and find or google. Short titles allow the reader to make a split-second decision on if he or she would like to preview your book. The book title is what will catch the reader's eyes and make them want to read the description of your book.

If you do not have a good title, then you will never be able to sell your E-book. You can do some testing by writing test E-books that you do not really want to sell and put them on sites and give them away for free. You should keep track of how many units each book gives away for free and the ones that are the most popular probably have the best titles and the titles are probably short and to the point.

I love to write "How to" books and so I like to include the words "How to" in the title of my book. For some reason, there are two catchy things that the reader really likes to have when they are selecting an E-book and that is the words "How to" and or the word "Guide." People love guide books because they always want to know how to do something so if you sell a guidebook people can benefit from it and learn how to do something they did not know how to do before. This will get people excited to be learning about something new and they will likely tell everyone they meet about your book so that you can sell even more books.

The name of your title is every bit as important as the content of your book. The title should have something to do with the content of your book because the last thing you want to do is misled a reader into thinking they are getting a book about autism when the book is about how to make money selling E-books. You want to be sure to make the title catchy and have very specific wording that will help the reader decide if they are interested in clicking on your book's description and reading more about it. If the reader does not click on the book description you might have a hard time selling any books. There is one exception and that is when you have the perfect title and the reader does not even take the time to read your book description they buy the book instantly and begin reading your story. Those sales are the best and easiest ones to get.

Selling books is something that takes a little bit of talent, a lot of time, and a lot of patience. You will not have a bestselling E-book overnight. That just does not make any sense and anything worth having in life is worth working for. It is important to stay passionate and keep fresh. Sometimes you will need to take a small break from writing for a few days. This does not mean that you are missing out on money or book sales because you have already produced your bestselling e-book and it is on the market for sale and you are making money from those books even while you sleep.

One of the coolest things as an author is the idea that you get to make money while you are sleeping. How many people can say that they have made money when sleeping? Think about that for a second. That is insane to know that you could make so much money from something you wrote two weeks ago, simply by going to sleep and allowing someone to buy it online really will blow your mind.

Self-publishing has become the new tradition for authors. There are now more E-books on the market than paperback books because of technology and it will not be long before all the leading traditional publishing houses are out of business. Traditional publishing was not set up to benefit authors, it was set up to benefit the publishers and make the publisher money.

Traditional publishers do not specialize in making books, they specialize in selling books. All a traditional publisher wants to do is pay you a small advance to have you create an amazing quality book for them that they know will sell. The issue is that these publishers are only publishing ten to twenty books per year and there are a lot of people who have stories written and ready to sell that are not getting their names out there because traditional publishing overlooked them because they were only interested in making money.

I really believe that all traditional publishers will be out of business by the year 2020. It is not going to take a lot more before the self-published authors are taking over the publishing industry. The nice thing about self-publishing is that you get to publish when you want, how you want, and where you want. The other amazing thing about self-publishing is that you get to publish as many books as you want and you can do it all on your own time frame. Perhaps an even better part to self-publishing is that you can do it from your computer at home in your pajamas like I am right now. I love having the freedom to be able to write where I want and when I want. Just being free to do whatever I want is really something that helps me and my writing. I work a lot better when I do not have deadlines from other people that I am trying to meet and self-publishing sure does beat trying to fill out the publication forms that traditional publishers want you to fill out before even submitting your manuscript for them to read.

It took me a while to understand publishing and to figure out that I could make money self-publishing. I made many mistakes and perhaps my biggest mistake was going with a vanity publisher that charged me

$4,000.00 to publish my first book. That is right I paid $4,000.00 that I had saved up over time to pay for the publication of my first book. Thinking back on that now I am wondering what I was even thinking. If I had known what I know now about the publishing industry there is no way I would have ever paid anyone a dime to publish my book because there is no need to. I can do it all from home right here sitting on my computer and I do not even need an editor because my grammar and spelling is good.

So now that we have picked a topic to write

about and we have been creative and come up with our title that is sure to catch people's eyes so that we can sell a lot of books we are ready to talk about the layout of your book.

3 LAYOUT OF BOOK

Different authors like to do things different ways and you are certainly welcome to come up with your own way of doing things and your own style. Please do not feel like you must lay out your book like I do but this book is laid out exactly how I lay out every book. I would recommend that you come up with one layout format that works for you and stick with it and use it for every book. It can become like your trademark and it can be a way for people to recognize your books and writing. It is very important for each author to have their own trademark in writing. I love to do chapter books and make chapters no matter how long or short the book is. I love to organize my thoughts into chapters. Each thought I have for the book is like a chapter in the book.

Just like when you choose the title of your book and then navigate the chapters to be about the title of your book you would want to title a chapter with a catchy name as well and then have the content of the chapter be all about the chapter that you are writing about. That all seems like common sense I am sure but I have read too many books over my lifetime in which the author did not even talk about or discuss anything related to the chapter of the book they were supposedly talking about. Please pay attention to detail when writing your book. You will want to put your best book out on the market because it is going to be on the market forever and people are going to be choosing whether they want to purchase your book or move onto someone else's book.

This goes without saying but it is also very important that your table of contents goes hand in hand with your content of the story because later we are going to talk about formatting and how to link the table of contents to the content of your story.

It will always be important to create quality content. The length of book should depend upon what you are writing about. I will say people like short stories now days that they can just pull up on their phone and begin reading while on the subway or waiting on an airplane. Some people even read E-books on the subway or airplane and they want to be able to start and finish a book within an hour or two. Traditional publishing mainly wanted long chapter books for so many years but with self-publishing the tradition of longer books is starting to become a thing of the past.

Traditional publishing usually required at least 80,000 words and often published books up to 110,000 words long. For self-publishing I try to keep most of my books under 20,000 words. I find that if we get too much higher than 20,000 words that the reader loses interest or may just not have time to be able to pick up the book and finish it. As I mentioned earlier a reader today likes the books that he or she can pick up and read in one setting. Most of my books I try to keep between 10,000 and 15,000 words for that exact reasoning.

The content of each chapter should contain a main paragraph that tells about the subject that you will be talking about and then it should also include several supporting paragraphs where you go into great- detail about the main paragraph and explain in more details what you are trying to communicate or get the reader to understand. This rule should apply to both fiction and non-fiction books. It can be very hard to keep a reader's interest if your supporting paragraphs do not have anything to do with the main paragraph in the section that you are writing about.

Keep in mind that your book is going to be for sale to all major retailers around the country and even the world. Someone in another country will be able to order your book and begin reading about your story. You have the power to reach a lot of people and you will reach a lot of people by using the right distribution channels. It is important that your book is of very high quality and that your content is full of facts for a non-fiction book or full of details about the characters and the plotline in fiction books.

I love to write short fiction stories that are about 5,000 words in length. There is enough content to tell a story but not too much content to where the reader gets overwhelmed with details about the story or the characters of the story. It is a lot of fun to write short stories in the genre of fiction and be creative. You should give it a try yourself because you might surprise yourself and have some of your best stories come from trying to throw together a fiction book on a whim.

I love to be creative. I find that there are a lot less rules and expectations involved when writing fiction. Do not get me wrong. I love to write non-fiction about topics that I am interested in but I feel like I am the freest to create content when I am trying to plot a fiction story in my head. I just let my brain think of details for the story as I type. Some of my favorite fiction works have come from when I was in a creative mood and did not put limitations or rules on myself when I was doing the writing. The best works are those that are created from the heart and mind. Whatever is in your heart it is probably something that you should be writing about daily.

I try to keep a journal of things that I like to write about. If a topic pops into my mind during the day I might just jot it down on a piece of paper or something. I take notes of things that I think about during the day and then at night when I am sitting by the computer I can process those thoughts and write about them to tell an amazing story.

Sometimes I will be doing something else and have a fiction story pop into my head that is so interesting I must take a break from whatever I am doing and get to my computer to write about it. It is very important that I get this idea to paper or to the computer now days so that I do not lose the inspiration for what I was writing about. Sometimes it is good to take your laptop with you wherever you may be going because if you find you are in the mood to write and have something you want to write about you will probably want to sit down and write it right away because that is when you will create your best content.

Now that we have the plan for the content we are writing about, the title of the book, and understand a little bit about how to layout content in the book we are ready to move on to the next part of our book. We are now going to talk about the book cover.

4 THE PERFECT COVER

Just as important as the perfect title is the perfect book cover. Your book cover will tell the reader a story and have them imagining what is going on in your book.

The book cover is something that will sell your book. The cover will make or break your book. If it is a printed book you will find that most people will not even pick up a book at the bookstore unless they like the cover or find the cover interesting. The cover is helping to pull the reader in and trying to get them to figure out what you are going to be right about. The best part of being a reader is that you get to take a picture and create a story in your mind and then read the author's story to see how close or different your stories compare to one another. I love to create stories in my mind based off book covers that I have seen over the years. Being creative and making stuff up is the best part of being a writer. You can spend your whole life writing non-fiction if you wanted to but you would be missing out on letting that creative person you have inside of you out and you would not be sharing it with the world. It is very important as people that we get in touch with our creative side.

There are several options to creating a book cover. My favorite is to Google noncopyrighted pictures and use them as the book cover and add some wording to them so that it looks like an official book cover. I have never run into any problems doing this and it is completely free. That is the best thing about making e-books. They are 100% free and you never must spend a dime to start making money. In fact, the book will make money for you for years after you release it and you will be able to sit back and relax and watch all the money rolling in.

It is important that the cover have

something to do with the book title and content in the book. For example, I am writing this book about how to make money writing e-books so I am going to likely use a book cover that shows money in it so people can correlate my book to something they need to read to learn how to make money and become successful or rich. People are going to be hooked by my book's cover and my book's title. If I can hook them in with one of those two concepts and get them to read the backmatter or description of my book, then

I will have a greater chance of them buying the book. Especially if my backmatter is good and tells part of the story to the reader that leaves them hanging and wanting to learn more.

You may be asking why a book cover is so important for an E-book. It is not like someone is going to physically see the book cover in person or touch the book cover but the book cover is something that is going to be used in marketing and promoting your books. If you do choose to do a paperback book you would want to use the same book cover for the E-book as you would the paperback book so that readers can connect the dots and you can sell both the E-book and the paperback book. Too often authors make the mistake of choosing different covers for the E-book and printed book and it ends up costing them a lot of money in sales.

Amazon also has a special deal where you can offer someone a free E-book with the purchase of a printed book of the same title or you can offer the E-book for a discounted price for someone who purchases your printed book.

I will always be a fan of a printed book and it is not a thing of the past, however, E-books are becoming more and more popular and printed books are going to be less and less from traditional publishers. Traditional publishing just cannot keep up with the self-publishing world and all the advancements that we have made with self-publishing. The E-book is so much more cost efficient and with distributors like Smashwords paying out higher royalties than the traditional publishing house it makes perfect sense why most authors have begun switching over to things like Smashwords to help get their stories out.

Smashwords is one of the greatest inventions in the world for authors. They not only sell your E-book on their website, but they also distribute your E-book to tens of retailers throughout the world. They distribute to Apple, Barnes & Noble, and many more. I have sold a ton of books over the past three years on smashwords and if you are reading this book then you too can make a lot of money selling books on smashwords and you are well on your way to doing just that.

So, use a picture for a cover that might tell a part of the book's story to the reader and get them imagining what the story might be about. If you can get their imagination going, then they are going to read the description or back matter so they can learn more about your book. Readers want to be hooked quickly because let's be honest we are all human beings and are attention spans are not very long. Therefore, it is even more important that your title and book cover picture hook the reader in and get them interested in learning more about your book.

5 BACKMATTER DESCRIPTION

Now that we have taken care of the book we must figure out a way to sell the book and market it. Getting the book uploaded to places where it will be marketed and viewed by thousands of readers is not very hard to do but you want to make sure that your story is well written and you have an awesome cover and title. Once you have those things in check it is time to write the book description that will go on the back cover and appear on the page where the book sells at places like Apple, Barnes & Noble, Smashwords, and Amazon.

There are going to be two descriptions that you right for Smashwords. Then there is going to be one main description that you right for Amazon. The Smashwords descriptions are very important as these are going to be distributed to multiple retailers. It is important to get your description perfect the way you want it before you submit your book for publication because once your book is published and approved for distribution changing your books description at retailers like Apple or Barnes & Noble could take weeks if not months.

I have toyed with putting excerpts from the books in my back matter or book description. Keep in mind that the back matter or back cover of the book is going to be a long description. Your short description is the thing that readers will see when they view your book in a list of books on an Apple website or a Barnes & Noble website.

The short description is probably the most difficult to write because you only have 400 characters that you are allowed to use. When you are writing the short description for Smashwords and its retailers you want to be very careful to make sure you end the sentence right at the 400-character mark or as close to it as you can be. It is important to use the full amount of space that you are given but it is even more important that you end with a sentence that has a punctuation mark at the end of it.

The short description might be shorter but writing the short description should take you just as long if not longer than writing the long description.

A simple trick for the long description is just to build upon what you did for the short description. I like to copy and paste my short description for my books and use them as my first paragraph for the long description. This way it is short and sweet and all I must do for my long description is add two or three more paragraphs to it to summarize my story. These descriptions are not meant to tell your complete story, they are meant to capture the reader's attention and allow the reader to want to learn more about your story and possibly purchase it from you.

Sometimes I find it useful to have a friend read my book and write my descriptions for me. I already know what the book is about and may have preformulated a certain summary that I want to give about the book. Another set of eyes might have something entirely different to say about your book in the book summary and you should always be looking for other people to read your writing and give you feedback on it as well. It is so important that you have more than one set of eyes read your writings. Someone else may be able to give you a summary that is better than what you could come up with on your own.

Sometimes I will even have two or three people read my books and write summaries for them. Then I will put all three of their summaries together and add and combine things to them to make one great big long summary for my book. It is so important that you have a well written and put together summary and it is important that it be right the first time before you submit your book for publication so that the readers will have a better understanding of what kind of book they are about to read.

Now that we have written the summary and done everything that we can do to put out the best quality product of an E-book we are ready to distribute and market. The next chapter will deal with sales and distribution.

6 HOW TO SELL YOUR E-BOOK

Writing the E-book was the easy part. Now that you have your book finished you are ready to sell it. How do you sell it? Luckily there are inventions like Smashwords and Amazon Kindle for independent self-publishers like you and me. We are very thankful to the people at Smashwords and Amazon who noticed a trend and need for a platform to publish and produce high quality E-books that we can write and sell or distribute with the help of Smashwords and Amazon.

I have a very specific routine when I upload my books. I always start out uploading my finished E-book to Smashwords first. I like going to Smashwords first because it will reach the most readers through Smahswords distribution channel. It may take a day or two before your book is approved for premium catalog acceptance and available at all the retailers but once it is available you will immediately see the benefits of publishing with Smashwords. In the meantime, you might even sell a few books directly from the Smashwords website like I have over the years. I love Smashwords.

After I finish uploading my book to Smashwords and have everything done there I choose to publish the printed version of the book with Create Space. The printed version of the book is an entirely different subject and something that I will cover in a different book. I will be making this book available as a printed book as well in the coming days.

I choose to go through Create Space to do the printed book simply so that I can get to the E-book version for Kindle with less work. Create Space has this amazing tool where once your printed book files are confirmed and accepted they will automatically turn your printed book into an E-book for Kindle. So, the first step is to go with Smashwords and upload your book there. Then once you have competed that go to Create Space. The nice thing about publishing on all these platforms is that you can copy and paste a lot of the details and summaries for your books. There is no need to sit and type out the long description or book summary repeatedly each time. In fact, the Amazon Kindle store will grab the long description of the printed book and pull it right into your E-book.

Create Space is a beauty and the best part about Create Space is that it takes care of the final step which is publishing your book on the Amazon Kindle. Once I have my book published and approved on Create Space it is automatically on the Amazon

Kindle and I do not even have to do anything except for go and set the pricing for my book.

There is a method I use to determine the pricing of my books based on the word count of my books. Amazon also has a tool where they will help you determine and set the price of your book for you based on what other books like your manuscript have been priced at. They usually set your price at the dollar amount that Amazon thinks you would sell the most books or make the most money at.

This is a great feature if you are new to publishing and do not understand the ins and outs of the publishing industry. It is also very important to begin to understand how self-publishing differs from traditional publishing.

The nice thing about self-publishing with Smashwords, Amazon, and Create Space is that they pay us a much higher royalty rate than traditional publishers would ever pay. Why is this nice you ask? Because that allows us to sell our books cheaper and make more money. Like for this book I am going to charge you $0.99 to learn about how to create E-books that sell and earn passive income for you. Who would not be thrilled to get a book this long and this in depth about a topic for $0.99. I recommend you study up on Smaswhords, Amazon, and Create Space to try and learn how their pricing and royalty payouts work. I will tell you for a book priced at $0.99 I will earn about $.60 cents per each book sold from Smashwords and about $0.35 per book sold from Amazon.

Amazon has different pricing percentages

for books $2.99 and over than they do for books less than $2.99. If you sell your book for less than $2.99 then you must accept the 35% payout instead of their normal 70% payout. Hopefully this is enough information to get you started on your way to publishing awesome E-books through Smashwords and Amazon. Try to check out Create Space along the way as well. The more platforms you publish your book on the more sales you will have. In this last chapter coming up we are going to address the pros and cons of using the Kindle Select programming that makes your book only available on Amazon for ninety days.

=

7 KINDLE SELECT

Your E-book is all finished and published.

You have done everything you needed to do

to make a great book that will sell millions

of copies. There is just one more

important decision left for you to make.

You need to choose if you want to enroll in

the Kindle Select programming that is

available to you. Kindle select allows more people to see and view your book and lets the reader view parts of your book.

It is a global fund that has a lot of money in it so that the authors all split the money based off a percentage of number of pages that someone has read of your book. I have used it before but I am currently not using it as I find there is more benefit to publishing my E-books on Smashwords immediately because Smashwords distributes to so many big retailers like Barnes & Noble and Apple. I feel the opportunity cost of missing out on Apple and Barnes & Noble sales is too great and I do not ever pass up the chance to publish my manuscripts on Smashwords immediately.

If you are a first-time author I do encourage you to try one book on the kindle, select plan to see how it does for you. You will just have to make sure that you do not publish that E-book anywhere else or on Smashwords for at least the 90-day period that you are enrolled in the Kindle select programming.

Thank you for purchasing my book. I appreciate that you all wanted to learn how to write an E-book that sells online. You are all now well on your way to earning passive income of up to $3,300 per month. Take care.

How to Make $3,300 per Week Writing E-books

ABOUT THE AUTHOR

I enjoy camping, hiking, backpacking, and traveling. I hope to visit all 50 states one day along with traveling abroad.

I like meeting new people so I go to new restaurants and hot spots throughout the city from time to time. I also have numerous online friends in which I stay in touch with through social networking sites like Facebook and Twitter.

I am a sports fan. Football and Basketball are my favorites. I play some recreational sports for fun only. I root for the IU Hoosiers, Boston Celtics, Green Bay Packers and Indianapolis Colts.

I have Asperger's which just means I'm Awesome.

My friend told me to write that. If you have questions about it, just ask me.

Having Asperger's also means that I'm nice, smart, super trustworthy, love to tell the truth, but I can sometimes seem a bit forward

T.B. McHatchins

BIBLIOGRAPHY

Comorbid Confusion

T.B. Shares about his life with comorbid autism and schizophrenia. Life is hard enough with autism but even more challenges present when you have schizophrenia. T.B. addresses some of the facts and myths of autism and mental illness and hopes to inspire the reader to understand people with the illness or developmental disability more. This is an educational book that will change the way you think.

In this book T.B. is very candid and open about things. He shares about his imaginary friends Tom and Red. He shares how he has hallucinations and even as he was writing a part of the book he was having a hallucination he was dealing with while writing. If you want a first hand account of what living with schizophrenia might be like then this is an excellent book for you to check out.

Towards the end of the book T.B. is diagnosed with Hydrocephalus and he writes about how all of these comorbid diagnoses confuse him and leave him wonder what symptom is caused by which disorder. The important thing is T.B. may be onto something with his hydrocephalus diagnosis and he feels more hopeful now than every before. From autism to hydrocephalus with schizophrenia in the middle T.B. takes the reader on a mental health roller coaster that is sure to keep you on the edge of your seat as you read.

T.B. shares how he has tried to remove his autism and cut it out because Red and Tom told him to do so. T.B. often listens to the voices because they only tell him to hurt himself. They say he must be punished for having autism but T.B. knows that they are lying and trying to get him to harm himself. Read this book to see how T.B. fights back against the hallucinations. Here is an excerpt from the book.

"One voice is named Red and another is named Tom. Both of these voices keep trying to tell me I need to cut the autism out of me. For some reason they hate my autism and say I have to get rid of it. There have been times where I have tried cutting with a razor to get the autism to bleed out of me. No matter how hard I cut or how many times I try I cannot get rid of the autism. I do not want to get rid of my autism but I feel like I need to in order to be safe and happy. The voices are completely against autism and they keep saying I am a bad person because I am autistic.

The voices are always out to hurt me because of my autism. They do not like it one bit and say that if I am ever without a neurotypical friend they will come find me and kill me. The voices are loud and clear even today as I type this. I do take several medications for them as mentioned earlier in this book. I try to block them out and I try to ignore them but it is very frustrating when people try and tell me they are not real and I should just ignore them.

Even my behavior consultant does not understand the voices and how they affect someone. He thinks they are not real and he says that I should be able to ignore them and just go on with life. I do not think he realizes how severe these voices and hallucinations are. The voices and hallucinations have ruined my entire life. I cannot even begin to function right now because I am hearing so many voices.

I have never been able to do well in college. I have never been able to keep a job for more than a couple months because of the voices. Everything about these voices is bad. I feel like they are out to kill me and sometimes it seems as if they are working with my doctor and autism support services staff to hurt me."

High Functioning Autism

T.B. describes what it is like to be forgotten by autism services because he is too high functioning. As high functioning as he is, he still has great difficulty in forming social relationships and keeping employment. He shares about how his staff is learning to help him day by day to be successful in employment and relationships. He is able to teach his staff his weaknesses and they work on them.

T.B, shares some tips and ideas for how you can help someone with high functioning autism or asperger syndrome like he has. If you are able to find a dedicated staff that is in it for the passion of helping adults that are high functioning can train their staff how to help them and teach them what they need to work on. It is a tragedy in the making that people who are high functioning are being ignored by the system and insurance companies. Ignoring the problem is only going to make it bigger and cost our country far more than it would have if we would have been providing great autism services for the higher functioning population.

T.B. discusses many similarities and difference between high functioning asperger syndrome and low functioning autism in this book. Someone who appears to be high functioning might not be any higher functioning than a lower functioning non-verbal person with autism. Just because they are verbal does not mean they know how to communicate. In fact, it is said that communication is ninety-three percent non-verbal and only seven percent verbal. You could imagine how confused someone with high functioning asperger syndrome would be by not being able to read any body language or non-verbal communication.

This book is sure to open your eyes to an end of the spectrum that is so often forgotten. This book also includes some fiction in parts of the story. Here is an excerpt from the book.

"But things still kept bothering me and I still had a very hard time making and keeping friends. I was working really hard at learning social skills and reading a lot of books. I am very good at researching and reading about things that I would like to know more about. So I try very hard to stay actively involved in the current literature as to what is out there.

Then all of a sudden when I was about 27 it hit me. I started hearing terrible voices that were saying such negative things about myself. They told me I needed to die and that I should self-harm as a punishment for being autistic. The voices did not like me and they were always mean and evil voices. Then I started seeing things and my illness was progressing. I saw people following me and chasing after me. I became frightened to even leave my home or go anywhere because I was afraid that someone was following me or chasing after me."

The Price of Being Autistic

T.B. McHatchins shares about being autistic and having to pay an "autism" bill to get other people to accept and like him. He grew up thinking that he was different and had to pay a price for being different. He paid people to sit next to them and class and gave girls hundreds of dollars just to go to dinner with him. It was not until he was in his thirties that T.B. begun to understand the truth.

T.B. does not discover that he has the talent, ability, and personality to get others to hang out with him without having to pay an outrageous fee for being different. Read along as T.B. learns how to love himself and overcome years of feeling like he had to pay an "autism" bill in order to get others to spend time with him. He goes from 0 friends with no money to a lot of friends with saving his own money for himself in this suspenseful book about a boy growing up with undiagnosed autism.

This book will teach self-esteem and confidence to other autistic children and adults. It is a great read for anyone wanting to gain a better understanding of autism spectrum disorder. T.B. shares very openly about how he used to sign his paychecks over to coworkers just so they would not make fun of him and bully hm. He shares how his best friends in high school made fun of him and pretended to tolerate him because of his disabilities. High school was devastating to T.B. and then he moved on to college where he thought it would be better.

T.B, goes through several more social rejections and paying his autism bill as well as finding out God hated him because of his disability. Although later in the story he learns that God does not hate anyone and in fact loves him very much. This is a story about a young man who is confused living with undiagnosed asperger syndrome learning to love himself and accept himself for who he really is.

Autism Love Bug

This fiction story of a man named Tom searching for love and finding it in unexpected places is sure to keep you on the edge of your seat wondering what Tom's next move is. Follow Tom on a quest to find love for someone who is a little different than most. Tom learns the skills to communicate who he is with women and finds they are more accepting of him when he loves himself with his whole heart.

Tom has autism. He has spent years and thousands of dollars paying people to teach him how to attract women. Nothing really helped and by the time Tom hit the age of 31 he was no longer interested in playing the games of dating. He wanted to meet someone true and real to marry and have children with. He decided the only way to do that was to be himself and not worry about his autism interfering with possible romantic relationships.

Tom decides to attend autism conferences all over the United States to find love. He hopes to meet like minded women who have autism or maybe a therapist or a single parent to a child with autism to fall in love with. While covering his booth and selling his books, Tom meets Jenna who opens up to him and tries to relate to him on a personal level. Tom is not used to this and jumps at the opportunity to talk to Jenna. Would he scare Jenna away like he does every other girl or would the two hit it off instantly and find they loved each other?

Autism Love Bug II

Jenna and Tom's remarkable love story continues with their engagement and wedding planning. Follow the couple as they have sex for the first time and become closer to one another throughout this book. Tom overcomes the challenge of his autism to meet, date, and possibly marry the women of his dreams. Will the ready go as planned without any roadblocks? You will have to read to find out the story.

Jenna and Tom are very good at being detail oriented. Planning weddings is stressful for anyone. Follow the couple in this thrilling book as they officially become boyfriend and girlfriend. Jenna moves in with Tom and the couple starts having regular sex that causes them to form an even closer bond. This book is an improbable love story of how a man overcomes the challenges of autism to date and possibly marry the woman of his dreams.

Will Tom and Jenna's wedding go off as planned or will there be a surprise that delays the wedding? Tom and Jenna spend every waking moment together except for when they are at work. Being apart for part of the day while they work proves to be healthy for their relationship. Tom plans the perfect engagement surprise for Jenna with both of their families being involved. This book is sure to keep you in suspense on the edge of your seat as you read. Will Jenna say I do? Or will something come up?

T.B. McHatchins

www.ingramcontent.com/pod-product-compliance
Lightning Source LLC
Chambersburg PA
CBHW070102210526
45170CB00012B/704